Stop Burning Your Money!

INTRODUCTION TO FINANTIAL FREEDOM

101

2ND EDITION

Proven Tips to Improve Your Financial Life and Sleep Better

JAVIER MATEO

INTRODUCTION TO FINANTIAL FREDOM 101

PROVEN TIPS TO IMPROVE YOUR FINANCIAL LIFE AND SLEEP BETTER

JAVIER MATEO

This book was published thanks to free support from:

Kinglionpublishing.com

Table of Contents

WHY I WROTE THIS BOOK

Why This Book is 100% GUARANTEED

Yes, order my new book for NOW. No strings. no catch. 100% GUARANTEED.

Truth be told. I'll probably lose tens of thousands of dollars by giving it away for such a low price. So WHY am i doing it?

Here's why: This isn't just my business. It's my passlon. My goal is to become THE worldwide spokesperson for fianncial freedom. I want this

message in this book in the hands of everyone. Not just those who are considering to buy it, but those who have never even

thought about it.

I want others to find that financial freedom and sense of purpose that they've always wanted. Be a success story! Then, years from now,

remember this powerful book that ignited this firestorm of peace.

The other reason I'm giving **INTRODUCTION TO FINANTIAL FREDOM 101**, 2nd Edition such a low price... because this model has already changed countless lives. Including

my own. Be the next person who's life is completely changed.

To No Catch, No Tricks, No Continuity Program

There is absolutely no catch here. There is no hidden continuity program. There is no trick or marketing gimmick.

1 slmply want to open up a relationship. Consider this Book offer like our first handshake. Of course, If more help & tools are needed in the

future... I would appreciate if people came back to my company to continue & furthur our relationship!

Believe me, there's no hidden agenda here. I simply want to start a relationship by offering to everything the tools that helped me build my

own success. Nothing more.

Why You Should Read This Book

NEW Book: PROVEN TIPS TO IMPROVE YOUR FINANCIAL LIFE AND SLEEP BETTER...
Introducing... INTRODUCTION TO FINANTIAL FREDOM 101- 2nd Edition

Over 10,000 People Have Read This Book

The Bestselling Book that's Changing mindset GLOBALLY!

Over 10,000 readers (and growing) have read this book in 2019.

But they didn't stop there. So many of these readers, even complete healthy financial habits.

Since that time, I've learned so much more about how to quickly and effectively PROVEN TIPS TO IMPROVE YOUR FINANCIAL LIFE AND SLEEP BETTER. Plus, we spent an entire year working with THOUSANDS of readers who gave us incredibly insightful feedback on our first edition.

With the combination of my NEW book and my readers, I knew I had to get a NEW and IMPROVED Second Edition of INTRODUCTION TO FINANTIAL FREDOM 101.

CHAPTER 1. FINANCIAL PLAN YOUR WAY TO SUCCESS

Financial planning is often considered a boring strategy used by our parents to manage our money. For a long time, financial planning was considered the way to manage one's money because it helped people keep track of money coming in and going out. But lots of people are choosing not to do any financial planning because it seems so needlessly complicated with little or not benefit.

Financial Plan

Financial planning is often considered a boring strategy used by our parents to manage our money. For a long time, financial planning was considered the way to manage one's money because it helped people keep track of money coming in and going out. But lots of people are choosing not to do any financial planning because it seems so needlessly complicated with little or not benefit.

But that couldn't be farther from the truth! There is a benefit to financial planning; the real trick is finding a financial planning method that works for you. Here is an excellent strategy to help you manage the money in your personal portfolio.

The first thing you need to do is create a financial plan. Creating a financial plan does not have to be restrictive, but it should be a guideline to help you manage your income and your expenses each month. The first thing you want to do is list all your expenses on a month-to-month basis. The next thing you want to do it list all of your income on a month-to-month basis. Then compare. Many people who have trouble saving find that their expenses are very close to their income. So what can you do?

One option you have is to reduce your expenses. This might mean going out with friends a little less or giving up on some luxury that you typically enjoy. Another option you have is to increase your income. Unfortunately, for many people, this is easier said than done.

One way that you can reduce your expenses and increase your income is by using a debt consolidation loan. By consolidating many outstanding debts that are due throughout the month into a single loan with a single monthly payment you will be accomplishing several things.

First, you will be reducing your monthly payment because you will be securing a larger loan and is spread out over a longer period of time. Second, you'll be reducing the amount of interest you pay because you will be consolidating your many debts into one debt from one provider. Reducing your interest not only helps to reduce your expenses but also increases your income!

And if you are able to find some assets that can help you get a UK Secured Loan, you'll be able to spread out your payment over a longer period of time and you will likely qualify for a lower interest rate because you have some security to offer the lending institution to back up the loan.

Now that you are actively pursuing a financial plan, you will need to find a way to continue to reduce your expenses over time. A UK Secured Loan will help you do that. But don't forget that there are many ways you can also increase your income.

Congratulations! You are assembling a financial plan and getting control of your finances and at the same time you are reducing your expenses and increasing your income.

Financial Checklist

To find out just what kind of financial shape you're in, answer the questions in the following Financial Fitness Checklist.1 If you're married, print this out and take it home so that you and your spouse can work together to answer the questions. Make a note of how many questions you answer yes to.

1. Are you using more and more of your income to pay your debts?

2. Do you make only the minimum payments due on your loans and credit cards each month?

3. Are you near, at, or over the credit limit on your credit cards?

4. Are you paying your bills with money intended for other things?

5. Are you borrowing money or using credit cards to pay for things you used to buy with cash?

6. Do you often pay your bills late?

7. Are you dipping into your savings to pay current bills?

8. Do you put off visits to the doctor or dentist because you can't afford them?

9. Has a collection agency called recently about overdue bills?

10. Are you working overtime or holding a second job to make ends meet?

11. If you or your spouse lost your job, would you be in financial trouble right away?

12. Do you worry about money a lot?

If you answered "no" to all questions on the Financial Fitness Checklist, you're the picture of financial health.

One or two "yes" answers, while not necessarily a sign of impending doom, can be a warning sign of potential problems. Before things get any worse, take time now to draw up a realistic budget (including a savings plan) or to revise your spending plan. Cut back on your use of credit cards, and watch closely for other signs of financial trouble.

Three to five "yes" answers could mean that you're heading for financial trouble. It's imperative that you get your spending under control right away. If you don't have a monthly budget, draw one up and follow it. Put away your credit cards and cut out all unnecessary spending until you can answer "no" to all the questions on the Financial Fitness Checklist.

If you answered "yes" to more than five of the questions on the Financial Fitness Checklist, you may already be in serious financial trouble. But don't despair. Financial counseling can start you on the road to financial recovery.

PERSONAL STEPS TOWARD REDUCED CREDIT CARD DEBT

The presence of multiple professional credit card debt management services nowadays are a testament of two things: (one) debt is a major problem in the financial industry, and (two) most people suffering from escalating debts cannot repair or settle those debts on their own. However, doing so is not entirely an impossible job provided that you remain dedicated in your effort to pay off any remaining debt and improve your credit report.

Settling Credit Card Debts On Your Own

One of the biggest dilemma that people had to face when it comes to hiring professionals in their credit card debt settlement or management is the additional charges involved. If you were trying to be practical, any additional cost is detrimental in your effort to free yourself from debt. Therefore, you need as much money as you can possibly find to resolve all of your remaining debt balances to your credit card company.

In fact, some people hire debt counselors or negotiators not to settle debts but provide debt settlement advices that you could probably figure out on your own. The approach at credit card debt settlement is pretty simply and straightforward, which is important if you want to embark on fixing your credit card debts on your own.

WHY ARE PROFESSIONAL DEBT MANAGEMENT SERVICES POPULAR?

One of the most evident reason behind the success of professional credit card debt management services is that they have the knowledge and willingness to negotiate a desirable deal. Professional debt negotiators are known to be capable of reducing debt balances by as much as 50 percent and they charge individuals with 15 percent of that fee.

One reason why professional debt negotiators are ideal for the job is that they are the bridge that brings together creditors and debtors in an agreed term. Meaning, debtors would be unable to settle those debts in the first place if not for the initiative of these professional debt management companies.

IMPORTANT FACTORS FOR DIY CREDIT CARD DEBT REPAIR

Before you try and find solution to your escalating credit card debts, there are a few compromises that you should be willing to take. After all, this is not a simple process given the stakes involved.

- You have to be willing to spend some of your time. Even professionals who do this on a regular basis know how difficult a task credit card debt repair is. You need to work on documents, communicate with your creditors, negotiate, and do a lot of follow-ups to ensure that the deal goes your way.

- You have to carefully thought out strategies that can be employed to achieve the result you want. This part of the process could be the most tiring.

- While trying to figure out what could work towards your advantage, you also have to identify the pitfalls you are trying to avoid.

- Establish realistic goals, such as being able to reduce (even in minimal percentage) your remaining balance. After all, you owe that money to the creditors so you have to pay what is due them.

How To Do it Yourself Effectively?

To attain better success with your doing your own credit card debt settlement, you need to document each step of the process. When you make payments, never do it over the phone or when you lack proper documentation. When releasing a statement to your creditor, always type them or have them handwritten so you have a written proof of any transaction that went on in your debt settlement process.

If you are suffering from a real financial hardship, use this as a turning point in your effort to seal a great deal for settling any remaining debts. Processing debt settlement yourself is similar to processing your own taxes or other professional or legal documents. If you have good negotiation skills, then use that to your advantage.

CHAPTER 2.

PRACTICAL CREDIT CARD DEBT SOLUTIONS

Improving your financial status and becoming free of debt usually only requires practicality on your part. When you learn to become responsible and practical in your use of credit cards, then you would not have had immense debt problems to begin with. However, you can apply the same level of practicality when it comes to paying off or settling debts.

Credit Card Debt Solutions

A few companies offer debt elimination programs but you need not jump right into it. You need to consider whether you will end up paying more than you could afford. However, if it saves you time and stress while also reducing the interest rate placed on your debts, then it would make great sense. There are steps that you can take yourself to advance toward your effort of becoming free of any credit card debt.

1. SET A SPECIFIC TIME FRAME FOR YOUR DEBT ELIMINATION.

Before you determine how much you are going to pay for your debt settlement on a monthly basis, you must come up with a specific time period first. Say for example, you are paying the minimum monthly payment for your debts, which means that you would end up paying your debt for another 5 or 10 years. If you want to shorten the payment period, then you can opt increasing your monthly payments if you do not want to extend your payment period.

2. Be Flexible with Your Debt Elimination Campaign.

In the middle of paying off your debts, it is not unlikely that some people with encounter financial emergencies. Therefore, it is best to opt for a credit company that allow flexibility or changes in your payment options when these cases should arise. Find a flexible debt payment plan that make room for such changes.

3. Determine Your Source of Cash for Purposes Outside Debt Settlement.

There are a few credit company that unable you to have access to your own money during emergency cases. Therefore, make this an important determiner when you look for a debt relief program. When you encounter financial emergencies, the inaccessibility of ready cash bring about more financial stress. Look for a debt settlement plan that will have extra funds available when such emergencies occur in the middle of working towards your goal to eliminate credit card debt.

4. Evaluate Its Impact on Your Credit Rating.

There are a few debt settlement methods that can impact your credit rating, so you have to find one that will help eliminate any of your existing credit card debts without necessarily hurting your credit status. If there are any negative marks that could tend to pull down your FICO score, look for other alternatives that could make your FICO score quickly increase. Whether it is making on-time payments or paying double the minimum monthly payments, you need to talk with your credit company to not just free yourself of any debts but also to boost your credit rating.

5. LOOK INTO ASSOCIATED FEES AND CHARGES.

Although some credit card debt elimination programs are offered for free, most are charged service. It is therefore important that you understand how much such services cost before you commit on your involvement with them. Some of the most common fees are upfront fees or attorney fees and some other processing charges. If there are any hidden fees, try to talk them out. The idea here is obvious: you are trying to lift off any financial burden and having your credit company charge you with huge amounts would not help at all.

Learning how to work your way around such negotiations involved with settling off credit card debts could help you be debt-free and regain better control over your finances.

Professional Credit Card Debt Management

CHAPTER 3.
PERSONAL FINANCIAL MANAGEMENT

When it comes to handling and managing finances, most people differ largely. There are those who can effectively do it on their own, while some others require professional help to get organized. Financial management already proves to be a difficult undertaking with the many financial considerations and budgeting involved. This is one of the reasons why debts, specifically credit card debts, is one of the leading problems in the United States alone.

Hence, many opt to seek out professional services in order to straighten out any financial shortcomings or overlapping debts.

Professional Credit Card Debt Management

Seeking the services of professional credit card debt management is a valid option for anyone wishing to get out of debt. The most obvious reason for this is that the people involved in this type of service deal with debts and other financial management services on a regular basis. Hence, their knowledge and expertise on the field can help you deal a more beneficial credit card debt management scheme.

Speaking of expertise, there are different types of professional debt management services that specialize on specific financial issues. Each one are designed in a specific method and objective such that not all types of professional credit card debt management services are suited for all. When you decide to partake in a given professional credit card debt management service company though, you have to subject yourself to the guidelines created by the company in the hopes of providing a limit to your spending.

BENEFITS OF PROFESSIONAL CREDIT CARD DEBT MANAGEMENT

Although you expect to settle some fees in accordance with the services provided, some people find it worthy for the set of benefits derived from acquiring professional debt management service. Here are just some of the most prominent benefits you can enjoy:

- With the services of a debt management professional, you can learn helpful tips and tricks when it comes to better financial and debt management. This provides a long-term benefit since you are able to practice healthier financial management methods that will (hopefully) keep you out of debt.

- You can save a large amount of time. You can use the knowledge of the debt management professional to know about the surest methods and techniques that you can employ to find debt relief.

- Depending on the type of service you hire them for, they can either process debt relief for you or provide invaluable advice that will get you out of debt.

- Simply put, hiring a debt management professional will help you secure a better deal.

TIPS ON CHOOSING SERVICES EFFECTIVELY

On top of the difficult decision on whether to hire a professional credit card debt management services comes the more difficult step in this entire process: choosing the service. With the wide array of debt relief companies in the industry and the presence of numerous scams, one could easily fall into committing mistakes.

Outlined below are some of the specific guidelines you need to consider before you can be confident that the professional debt management service you hired is one to take you out of debt.

- Perform a thorough research. This is beneficial not only in terms of comparison but also in ensuring that your debt management service is legitimate.

- Compare what you can gain from the service and the costs charged for that service.

- Opt for a credit card debt management company who has established a good reputation in the business.

CHAPTER 4.

BE SUCCESSFUL

You have probably heard the term "IQ" many times, and you probably know it has something to do with measuring intelligence.

The letters "IQ" stand for "intelligence quotient", and an IQ test is widely used as a way to measure intelligence.

The test most frequently used today to measure intelligence is called the Stanford-Binet Intelligence Test. The earliest version of it was developed in France in 1905.

Do You Need to Have a High IQ to Be Successful?

The original test has been revised several times over the years, with a major revision completed at Stanford University in 1960. The Stanford-Binet test is not the only intelligence test, but it is probably the best known.

IQ tests are often used by educational institutions to segregate students into categories such as "normal", "gifted", and "challenged".

Children and young people are scored relative to each other on a variety of factors, including verbal and logical understanding, vocabulary, arithmetic and spatial orientation.

A person with an IQ score of 100 is deemed to be of average intelligence, while a person with an IQ above 130 is deemed to be intellectually gifted.

Although the IQ test is very widely used, and the results are almost synonymous with our idea of intelligence, there has also been a lot of criticism of the test, and of the way the results are used.

Does having a high IQ score guarantee success in later life? No, it doesn't! It doesn't even guarantee success in school.

A Canadian television program recently tracked down some of the people with the highest IQ scores in North America.

One man who has an extremely high genius IQ works as a motorcycle mechanic, hangs out with biker gangs, and is frequently in and out of jail.

Another man interviewed on the program has the highest IQ recorded in North America. He has worked as a bouncer in a bar for ten years, earns minimum wage, and lives in a tiny garage. Clearly, a high IQ is not enough to guarantee success in life.

What IQ tests measure is a certain type of potential. That potential still needs to be developed and nurtured by the person who has it. That person may not have the inclination or desire to do so.

Not everyone who has a potential talent also possesses the desire to do something with it. One person may have a wonderful God-given singing voice, but may have no interest in music, and no desire to perform.

Another person may have the perfect physique to be a high jumper, but may hate sports. You can probably think of other examples. Having potential is just a beginning.

The IQ tests we have now may predict which people have a certain type of intellectual potential, but they don't necessarily predict who will become a good teacher, a good manager, a good president, or a good parent.

Some critics say that the only thing IQ tests can really predict is who will do well on IQ tests.

Qualities such as determination and vision can be more important to your ultimate success in life than the IQ number you started out with. Being creative, optimistic, and flexible are important hallmarks of many successful people.

Common sense, the ability to get along with other people, and knowing a good idea when you see one, may be more useful qualities than having a genius IQ.

Five Steps To Success In Everything You Do

If you follow these 5 steps, no doubt you will get everything you want!

1.	What you need first is to have a strong desire. A desire like a fire! Not like a little flame you have to stir to get some heat going. No, you need a strong desire, you must really want to have what you long for! If you want something badly, but you didn't get it until now, it is your desire was not strong enough! You must really feel the desire to have it in your bones, in your flesh, in your heart. The desire is the starting point, because without passion nothing can happen.

2.   Now you need to set goals. Why? To know where to go! Without goals your desire will get you nowhere and you will turn around in circles like a dog who runs after his own tail. A goal gives you a reason, a purpose. The word goal means to GO ALl the way to get there! Your goal is your direction where your desire will take you. If you're able to see with your mind's eye what you want, you will have it. So the more details you see, the more concrete is your mental image, the more likely you will get exactly what you long for! Goals get your energy running. Goals generate the necessary activity to bring you towards the realization of your dream. A good goal is a statement of what you want, in a positive, clear, concrete way and with emotion (remember the fire! Without emotion, without fire, no outcome!). A goal should be written down, to give it more energy, and should be stated in the present time. You write your goal down as if you got it already. And start to act as if you were

already there!

3.   You must believe in yourself. You must really be conscious of the fact that you are worth to have what you desire and that you are able to get it, that you got everything you need to realize your dream. Yes you can! Maybe you do not know for now how to get there, but believe in the fact that you will learn step by step how to do it and that you will be guided on your way by coïncidences and syncronicity.

4.   A strong desire, a clear positive goal, a strong believe in yourself, what else does it need to make your dreams come true? Positive thinking! The most beautiful dream, the strongest desire and the clearest goal will bring you nowhere if you destroy yourself with a negative belief system. If you have this lousy habit of seeing everything rather black than white, of fearing the worst, of expecting bad things to happen, this mindset will bring you what you ask for : black, fear, bad. A positive mindset lifts you up to the

evel of universal creation and the universe will conspire with you to give you what you long for.

5.	Consistency. Yes, it is easy to start things. It is easy to quit. But it takes consistency to stay on your road. Did you ever taste the freedom which lies in the fact that, after years and years of practicing the same thing, you became an expert in something? With your eyes closed you can answer any question on the subject and produce almost any result you want? You are an expert now because you did the same thing hundreds of times, over and over again. And now you know! What a freedom! Consistency, not giving up, always going on in the same direction, this brings you freedom at last. Why? Because you don't need to think and to search anymore on your subject. It became a habit and you have space free in your mind to learn new more demanding stuff. Stay on your road, go on and on, every step will take you to more freedom, happiness and mastery of your life!

These are the five crucial steps to succeed in whatever you want.

How Do People Become Successful?

Here's an interesting fact you may not know about. In America, there is a millionaire made every 5-10 minutes! And here's the most surprising thing. Most of these millionaires (around 80%) either didn't finish college, came from poor families or didn't even speak English as their first language!

So when you actually look at who millionaires are, you realize that virtually all of them started out as ordinary people just like you and me. So if they did not come from rich families or win the lottery, how did they do it?

Well, millionaires became millionaires by learning the skills needed to make them rich. This shows us success is just a skill that anyone can learn,

regardless of how well you did at school. If you are willing study success and
discipline yourself to apply the knowledge you have learned, then you could
also become a millionaire.

LEARNING THE SKILLS OF SUCCESS

So why should you learn about success anyway? Well, think about when you
first started driving. What did you have to do? You booked an instructor, and
learned how to drive a car from someone who was already good at driving.
In other words, you learned a new skill from a person who already had that
skill.

But now suppose you decided you didn't need an instructor and decided to
take to the road by yourself, learning things as you went along. Can you
imagine what would happen?

Well, if you didn't first get pulled over by the police, there would be a fairly
good chance you would either a) crash or b) have an accident! Can you see
where I am going with this?

Success, just like driving is a skill. Those who learn about success get to
where they want to go, those who don't learn the skills of success crash on
their way. It really is that simple.

OBSTACLES TO SUCCESS

In ancient times people used to think that the Earth wasn't round. So most people made sure that they didn't sail very far because they were afraid that if they did, they would fall off the Earth! Today we know this as the flat Earth theory.

However it was soon discovered the Earth was not flat, but in fact it was round! When people heard about this they were no longer scared about failing off the Earth, and so began to sail to new and far away lands.

This story is a great example of how what we believe to be true can either limit our life, or expand it. It also shows us that if you want to go somewhere you first have to believe that you can do it. In other words, our belief systems greatly influence the world around us and ultimately the success we will achieve.

So the two important points to take away from this article are:

1) Success is just a skill. If you learn that skill you can become successful regardless of who you are.

2) Your beliefs play a big role in determining the type of success you will achieve.

So, achieving success is quite simple. Learn from people who already have the skills of success and believe that you can achieve success. However, this does not mean things will be easy!

Chapter 5.
Legal Action When Choosing To Not Pay Any Money

Legal action should be expected for anyone who is avoiding paying their monthly debt each month, by one creditor or another or more than one at a time even. You never know how bad it could get if you just let all of your debt go for so long, you could find yourself being sued by some of your creditors and if that happens you will have no choice but to somehow come up with the money that is needed to pay off some of those debts, whether you like it or not.

There is simply no way for anyone of you to avoid any sort of legal action whenever you are choosing to just not pay any of your debt that has been accruing now for so long. Once legal action has begun there is normally no other way for you to get out of having to pay off your creditors, unless there is some sort of prearrangement made by both you and your creditor but that arrangement has absolutely got to always be accomplished monthly and on time.

You have a responsibility whenever you purchase something via your favorite credit card or however you are choosing to make the purchase on some type of credit. Too many people are running up their credit cards and some people actually know up front that there is never any way possible that they will ever have the ability to pay off any kind of debt such as credit cards.

If you can come up with some type of financial plan for yourself and for the future of your children then you will be much better off in the long run. There are financial advisors in your local bank branch or you could find yourself one on the internet, that could provide you with plenty of helpful information regarding debt and all of the different things you can do to help your current situation that you have gotten yourself into throughout the years.

Take full responsibility for every action that you make, especially your financial choices. By doing so you are going to be teaching all of your children the appropriate way to handle their finances as they grow older into adulthood. You can teach them helpful things about not acquiring too much debt as they grow older and you will really be providing them with the most beneficial advice possible.

Allow them to ask you questions about debt and anything concerning it, so that they can gain more and more helpful knowledge from their intelligent and very wise parent, that they will thank and look up to forever because of such love and tremendous guidance. Debt does not have to be a big bad monster, if you can control your spending and be smart with all of your choices, along with keeping up on all of your monthly payments, your finances should remain in place and your future seems bright.

Find Out More About Improving Your Credit Score-Debt Does Not Have To Create So Many Problems For You

Trying to make improvements that will reflect on your credit score is a very wise decision, especially if you can do it early on enough for it to really make a big difference with your financial status. Throughout this article I want to discuss with you all some very important information regarding debt and how to get rid of it, so that hopefully you will be able to correct some of the mistakes that you have made over the years.

So many problems can be created because of ruining your debt and of course your credit score, early on in your life. You do not want to have to deal with this kind of problem, really you don't. If any little change can be made that might provide you with some financial comfort or relief, then please start working on those things immediately because if you do not then your financial future might potentially have such an enormous strain on it that there really is nothing that you could possibly do to make anything any better financially.

Your credit score actually provides all of your credit history to any creditors checking into it. Anything that you decided not to pay or just simply could not pay, it will all definitely show up, reflecting very poorly on you at some point in time for whatever reasons you might be trying to get some sort of loan or establish yourself as a reliable, responsible adult who pays their bills in a timely manner and can be trusted completed when agreeing to pay some type of debt in the future.

Any sort of financial mishap or serious debt issue, can totally destroy your chances of having the ability to purchase certain things throughout life, which can really put a big damper on many different things. Your debt condition can cause so much stress that you end up with serious health issues, this is something else that you should most definitely consider right now, instead of later on in life. Debt does not have to be so terrifying because if handled properly there are many things that you can do to make simple corrections, which will relieve you from a large strain that you have accidentally gotten yourself into.

Improving your credit score can be done by many different means and you will find it to be most beneficial, after only working on it for just a short amount of time. Do not expect it to happen overnight because it does not work that way, however, it will not take as long as some of you might have first expected. Be patient and persistent, as well as consistent, when it comes to improving the way that you spend your money and save your monthly excess of cash flow coming in and it will work out for you.

Debt does not have to destroy your life but if you choose to just let things go, over a period of time, it can and will happen to you, nobody is safe from the debt monster.

Debt Can Eat Away At You Over The Years-Find Out What You Can Do To Stop This Cycle

Over abundance of debt can totally creep up from out of nowhere for many people and when that does occur it can often times be very overwhelming for many. It is so very important for everyone to keep in mind how very important it is to always try and steer clear from too many unwanted debts because all that leads to is stress, stress and more stress, which far too many of us know a little bit about, or maybe even a whole lot about.

If your debt condition is currently driving you up the wall then you already know how devastating it can turn out to be, so make sure even you continue to read throughout this article because you might find it to be very helpful, as well as beneficial to you. Your debt responsibilities will become a priority and you will finally have the opportunity to get yourself and your financial standing on the path that it should be, which is where most of us only dream of ever having it.

It is your responsibility as an adult to start thinking more about the future of yourself and the future of your children as well, which I am certain most of you already have given thought to. Finding out more about the importance of debt relief will change the way you live your life each and everyday that passes. You will be much more conscious about the different things you are spending your money on, as well as the amount of money you are trying to save each month, if any at all.

Your money should be very helpful to you but if you constantly are finding out that your money seems to be going nowhere except to pay off your monthly debt, whenever you are able to, then perhaps something within your budget could need some improvement, just a little bit. I am hoping that by gathering up enough debt information you will be able to finally get your finances under some sort of control and stop increasing your debt each month.

Debt can be controlled by just making a few small changes in your lifestyle each month and I am not at all talking about anything major that would affect your entertainment each month or fun times with friends. Just slow down and pay closer attention to what is coming out of your wallet and if you can continue this type of responsible behavior over a period of time then you will definitely begin noticing slight changes in the amount of extra money you have each month.

If all else fails, talk to a professional about your current debt condition and there is surely to goodness somebody out there more experienced and knowledgeable than you are, who could really help to turn your world around, by providing you with the same knowledge that they are aware of because of studying it over a period of time throughout life. This knowledge can be a lifesaver and can really brighten the outlook of your future, as well as your children's and grandchildren's future. Good luck.

CHAPTER 6.
MANAGE YOURSELF

A Golden Rule To Manage Job/Workplace Stress: Having gone for a sea bath, don't be afraid of the oncoming waves. Take your plunge!

* Getting a job, involves lots of stress.

* Getting a job, without the stressful environment, is a blessing.

* Getting a job, with the type work profile that you like, a cheerfully disposed staff, and the administration that maintains the human relations at its best, is a boon!

A Golden Rule To Manage Job/Workplace Stress

You put in your best efforts, but everyone around you is dissatisfied. The reasons are beyond your understanding. Your fellow-workers are not happy with you; some of them do not hesitate to taunt you. Your boss frowns at you for nothing. Your wife nags you for your late arrival by 30 minutes from the office. Traveling through public transport, leaving your kid to school, going to the market in between hustle and bustle of office and home-what more is required for you to say, 'oh, this hellish life!'

These are some of the issues that contribute to your job workplace stress.

If someone else is to be blamed for your stress, blame yourself much more for giving that prominent place for the Satan of stress. Throw him out lock, stock and barrel from your personality. Take a firm stand. Yes, it is possible; it is achievable.

A story goes thus: An educated youngster, fed up of his job workplace stress, ran away to Himalayas. There he met a Yogi. The youngster prostrated at his feet with all humility, and prayed that he wants to stay at His hermitage, as he was fed up of the city life and the job workplace stress.

Yogi's reply was historic: Don't runaway to any Ashram; create an Ashram, where you are!

What you need to to is to analyze and understand your stress. Take out the negativities one by one. Unburden the burden! Mind in itself, doesn't have any existence. It is supposed to be a bundle of thoughts. Take out the thoughts, one by one and reduce the heavy load that you unnecessarily carry on your head.

There was another young man who wanted to take a bath in the sea. He stood at the seashore all the time worrying- let these waves disappear from the ocean, then I will take bath. Will that situation ever be possible? The message to such an youngster would be- having gone for a sea bath, don't be afraid of the oncoming waves. Take your plunge!

With a positive bent of mind it is possible to control and transcend job workplace stress. Stick to your job, have patience and understanding! Go placidly amidst the noise and din. Everything is happening, as it should!

A Guide To Performance Management

Nowadays, a great significance is being given to Performance Management, as companies incorporate them in their effective management strategies. However, a lot of people find this process a complicated one, mostly because of the many options that it offers – on the organization, a specific department/branch, a product or service, and on employees, among others.

In order to minimize this confusion, the items below will give you a general idea of what Performance Management is all about as well as the activities that are involved in this process.

WHAT IS PERFORMANCE MANAGEMENT?

Performance management is a process that provides both the manager and the employee (the person being supervised) the chance to determine the shared goals that relates to the overall goals of the company by looking into employee performance.

WHY IS IT IMPORTANT?

Performance Management establishes an outline for employees and their performance managers to assess and to come to an agreement on certain concerns and aims that are in accordance with the overall structure of the company. This enables both parties to have clear objectives that would help them in their work and in their professional growth.

WHO CONDUCTS PERFORMANCE MANAGEMENT?

Performance Management is carried out by those who oversee the performance of other people – work/team leaders, supervisors, managers, directors, or department chairs.

What are the processes involved?

Below are the phases of the Performance Management process:

1. Planning

This phase of Performance Management process includes establishing job descriptions and identifying the employee's essential functions as well as defining the strategic plan/s of the department or the company as a whole.

Job Description

A job description is used to advertise a vacant position, which typically specifies the following:

- The specific functions, tasks, and responsibilities of the position

- The amount of time needed to act upon each function

- The qualifications needed (skills, knowledge and abilities) to perform the job

- The physical and mental requirements of the position

- Salary range for the position

- To whom the position reports

Job descriptions should be disclosed to the employee as soon as he or she is hired. Note, however, that job descriptions are listed using words that make it difficult to measure the employee's performance. They are in contrast with competencies, which list the skills needed in performing such tasks and are described using terms that can be measured.

Strategic Plan

In effect, a strategic plan tells you three things:

- Where the company is heading in the coming year/s.

- How the company is going to get there.

- How the company will know if it is already there or not.

Included in a strategic plan are the following:

Mission statement – the primary reason why your department (or company) exists.

Goals – associated with the mission statement, they determine the results that will advance said statement/s.

Strategic initiatives – specifies definite steps that must be taken to accomplish each goal. It is a dynamic process, usually examined during periods such as one or two years.

2. Developing

This phase of Performance Management process includes developing performance standards, which offers a scale that describes how a specific job should be performed in order to meet (or exceed) expectations. They are explained to newly hired employees and are later used to evaluate work performance.

Performance standards are generally outlined with the help of the employees who actually perform the tasks or functions. There are a number of advantages with this approach:

- The standards will be suitable to the requirements of the job

- The standards will be applicable to actual work conditions

- The standards will be easily understood by the employee (and performance manager as well)

- The standards will be acknowledged (and received) by the employee and the performance manager

Standards of performance are usually in the form of ratings (1 to 5, A to E) that are used by performance managers to rate the employee's actual level of performance.

3. Monitoring

This phase of the Performance Management process includes monitoring employee's work performances and giving feedback about them.

As the basis of feedback, observations should be verifiable: they should involve noticeable and work-related facts, events, behaviors, actions, statements, and results. Feedback of this type is called behavioral feedback, and they help employees improve and/or sustain good performance by precisely identifying the areas that the employee needs to improve without judging his or her character or motives.

4. Rating

This phase includes conducting performance evaluations. This is the critical aspect of the Performance Management process, especially because it is important for performance managers to arrive at an unbiased assessment.

A performance appraisal form has the following features:

- Employee information

- Performance standards

- Rating scale

- Signatures

- Employee performance development recommendations

- Employee comments

- Employee's Self-appraisal

Why conduct performance appraisals? It provides an opportunity to improve performance in the future not only for employees, but for managers as well. Performance appraisals enable managers to acquire information from employees that will help them make employee's jobs more productive.

5. Development Planning

This phase of the Performance Management process includes establishing plans for improved employee performance and development goals. This advances the overall goal of the company and at the same time increases the quality of work by employees by:

- Encouraging constant learning and professional growth.

- Helping employees maintain the level of performance that meets (and exceeds) expectations.

- Improving job - or career-related skills and experience.

In closing, Performance Management is a process that, when executed fairly and effectively, can improve the quality of the company's workforce, raise standards, increase job satisfaction, and develop professionalism and expertise that would benefit not only the employees but the entire organization as well.

Chapter 7.
Talking About. Numbers

Accounting Professionals: Are They Necessary?

Does your business needs an outside accountant?

It all depends. If you require an audited or reviewed financial statement, then, yes, you need a CPA. In any event, it is always a good idea to maintain a relationship with an accountant no matter how small your business. Whether your accountant is a CPA is up to you. The real question is: To what extent do you need outside accounting services? That also depends on you and the nature of your business.

I always start with the admonition: The Buck Stops With You! You cannot afford to dissociate yourself from understanding the meaning of your financial statements. If you solely rely on your accounting staff or accountant for completely accurate financial data, then you are asking for trouble. If you are going to own or manage a business, then you have a responsibility to learn how to speak the language of business. The language of business is accounting knowledge.

How involved you become in the accounting process will be determined by time schedules, your mental pre-disposition, desire for control, cash flow, etc. One scenario, if you can afford it, is to hire an internal accounting staff to prepare financial statements on a monthly basis and have an external accountant check them over. Another common scenario is to prepare part of the compilation yourself, such as preparing a sales journal and a cash disbursements journal, and then hire an outside accountant to prepare a bank reconciliation and the financial statements for you. Some do this on a monthly basis, others quarterly. Some business owners do the books themselves all year and turn them over to the accountant at the end of the year to verify the balances and do the depreciation entry for tax purposes.

There are numerous ways to work with an accountant. Regardless, you should learn enough about accounting to be able to communicate intelligently with your accountant. Since you are intimately involved in your business you may recognize danger signals that not even your accountant will see.

Selecting an accountant

Relying on the yellow pages to find an accountant can be risky. The best way to find any professional is by a referral. However, you need to interview prospective accountants before signing on. One of the first priorities is to find out what their experience level is. Your business may have very specific accounting and tax issues that require a certain amount of expertise. Perhaps you have a manufacturing concern. What does the accountant know about raw materials, work-in-process, and finished goods inventory accounting? Does the accountant know how to set up job-costing and overhead burdens? Ask for references from other like-kind businesses.

Keep in mind, that you may go to an established firm with a good reputation, but with whom are you going to have a relationship? Is your account large enough to warrant a relationship with a partner? You need to feel confident with the person assigned to your account. Perhaps a smaller firm with four or five accountants who are all seasoned veterans might work better.

You will also want someone with whom you can relate. The ability to communicate is a crucial factor. Your accountant may be technically proficient but can you understand what he or she is telling you? Does he or she listen when you ask questions? Don't be afraid to ask for someone else if you are having difficulty communicating.

Another important criterion is "accessibility". Is your accountant too busy to talk to you? Can you get your questions answered within a reasonable period of time? Do you feel important to him or her? Situations may arise where you need information immediately to make an important business or tax decision, will your accountant respond quickly?

Last, but not least, are the accountant's billing practices. Billing practices vary from firm to firm. Some firms are very aggressive and put tremendous pressure on staff and partners to bill every minute they can. Some firms require a review process before any work goes out the door. This means that every person who performs any work on your account, including the person who puts the stamp on your envelope, bills you for it.

Find out in advance what happens if you call the firm to ask a simple question that takes less than five minutes to answer. Are you billed for five minutes or are you billed in increments of fifteen minutes even though you only talked for five? Some firms justify this increment billing by explaining that you are paying for the accountant's expertise that may have taken years to acquire, therefore, they say, it's worth it.

Some accounting practitioners charge a flat rate for services rendered or a combination of flat services and hourly charges. For instance, an accountant might charge $200 a month to prepare a monthly financial statement but charge $100 an hour for special projects. Within the monthly fee, the client can call to ask questions that last fifteen minutes or less for no additional charge. This way the client is not reticent about calling. Getting your question answered may prevent little problems from later becoming bigger more expensive problems.

Very often projects take longer to complete than anticipated. Complications arise and the practitioner should be paid for his or her work. Always insist that, if there are going to be additional charges over and above what has been agreed upon, that the accountant gets your approval first. Be sure to clarify these procedures before engaging an accountant in an "engagement letter". This is a document that spells out the responsibilities of both parties and how the relationship is going to work.

Remember, there is absolutely no reason to be intimidated by your accountant. After all, you are paying for the services, and I promise you, the accountant wants your business.

4 Money-Saving Tips For Every Homeowner
Chapter Text

Losing weight. Finding a new job. Spending more time with the family. A new year means setting new goals. Why not make saving money one of them?

If you're a homeowner, there are many ways you can cut costs and still live comfortably. The following tips will help lead you to financial success.

* First, set a budget. Figure out exactly how much you spend on the upkeep of your home. Compare each month's expenses with the previous month's to get a better idea of how much to budget for each necessity. Then, see what costs you can cut. Once you set a budget, stick to it.

* Save energy. You might be losing a substantial amount of energy dollars during the winter and summer because of air leaks. By caulking, sealing and weather-stripping all cracks and openings, you can save 10 percent or more on your energy bill.

Also, look into replacing older appliances with newer, more energy-efficient alternatives. Your light bulbs can make a difference, too. Fluorescent bulbs are four times more energy efficient than incandescent bulbs.

* Refinance. Shop around to see if you can replace your existing home loan with one that has a lower interest rate. You can easily save hundreds of dollars each month by refinancing your home.

* Purchase a home warranty. Most homeowners don't account for possible repairs in their annual budget. There is a 68 percent likelihood of a home system or appliance failure in a given year. The average replacement cost of one of these systems or appliances is $1,085. A home warranty is your best defense against unexpected and costly repairs to your home's appliances and mechanical systems.

The American Home Shield Home Warranty, for example, ensures you get the best possible service through the company's network of pre-screened technicians. The minute something breaks down, you can contact American Home Shield and a local service technician will schedule an appointment that fits your schedule. The warranty covers a multitude of household systems and appliances, regardless of age.

The American Home Shield Home Warranty is a one-year contract that requires no home inspection to enroll. Several affordable plans are available to fit every budget.

About Dormant Bank Accounts

Banking experts estimate that up to £5bn may be sitting unclaimed in UK bank accounts that have gone 'dormant'. What does this mean, and could you be entitled to a share in this huge amount of idle money?

A bank account goes dormant when, in the words of the British Bankers' Association, a bank and a customer 'lose touch with each other'. What this usually means in practice is that a customer has either passed away or moved house, and the bank haven't been told and are unable to locate the account holder some time later.

If there are no transactions on an account over a period of around 12 months, the bank will write to the account holder at the last known address to ask them if they wish to keep the account open. If no reply is received, then the bank will change the status of the account to 'dormant'. This means that from now on, no statements, chequebooks or other correspondance will be sent out to the customer.

The money in the account will still earn interest at whatever the normal rate of that account is, and the bank will still keep track of the account balance and keep a record of the last known address of the holder.

There are two main reasons for an account being made dormant. The first and most obvious one is to save the banks the administration costs of sending out statements and the like when there is no activity on the account from month to month (other than that initiated by the bank itself, such as interest payments).

The more important reason however is to guard against identity fraud. If a bank continues to send statements to an address when the account holder is no longer there to receive them, it is all too easy for these documents to end up in the hands of fraudsters, who could use the sensitive information they contain to begin a campaign of ID theft.

Most dormant accounts will have very small balances, but some will inevitably contain a substantial sum, often those belonging to someone who has passed away. If you think you may be entitled to money held in a dormant account, you can make a claim by filling in a form available from the bank in question.

You will need to give your reasons for making a claim, such as that the account belonged to a close relative whose estate was passed to you. You will also need to prove your own identity, and your connection to the original account holder if applicable.

If the bank don't agree that you're entitled to take over the account, you have the right to pursue an appeal, where your claim is re-examined. If the appeal fails, you can take your claim to the Financial Ombudsman Service, whose decision is final and binding.

CHAPTER 8.
PERSONAL FINANCE IS YOUR RESPONSIBILITY

Whether or not you choose to ignore it, you cannot deny the truth embedded in this statement: Your personal finance is and always will be your responsibility.

When it comes to finance, many people put an impractical blind eye to the fact that finances need to be managed. Personal finance is an ever-growing popular term for adults and teenagers alike, regardless of whether you are earning the money or not. After-all bills have to be paid, family members have to be fed and your lifestyle has to be maintained.

Personal Finance

The biggest and most neglected step for many families is teaching their teens how to manage their money. Teenage finance is about educating teens on the value of money. Teach them how to save by showing them how to use their primitive form of book-keeping. This can often be incorporated through the child's upbringing via

piggy-banks, savings accounts, and little chores in exchange for money.

Teenage finance is an important part of your personal finance because, too. When your children learn to save and use money wisely, you are subsequently saved from bailing them out of financial troubles in the future.

Personal Ethics and finance go hand-in-hand; if you have a good relationship with yourself, you will be able to save money. You won't feel the urge to do things that go against your ethics like sign-up for a credit card using someone else's name.

Personal finance involves taking a few steps toward safe-guarding your money. Your money spent should not exceed your money received. In order to prevent this from happening, you should make a crude balance sheet and use it to record all of your transactions.

Each month write down how much was received and how much was spent. Make a list of all the things the money was spent on, so you can keep track of your money.

You will be amazed at how much we spend on things that are not necessities.

Make a list and stick to it. Always try to get the best deal for your money and remember that cheaper does not necessarily mean lower quality.

After-all it is your money; managing your personal finances should be seen as a mandatory part of making money work for you.

ABOUT THE AUTHOR

Javier Mateo he is one of the most important authors of *KING LION PUBLISHING* editors. its purpose is to ensure that at least one hundred thousand people achieve a full life economically with their recomements and experiences..

for authors at Kinglionpublishing@gmail.com

Thanks again for your support!

Free Bonus

Mortage loan Excel template

Annuality investment Excel template

Retirement planner Excel template

Conventional Mortage Excel template

Daily planner Excel template